Step-Dads are **Special**

And Mine is the **BEST**

Hi! I'm Jarvis and I'm eight years old. This book is about my dad.
He's a pretty special guy as you are about to find out.
My dad is really my step-dad. That means he's not my real dad.
But, he's my real dad to me.
The only thing that is "step" about my dad is that he stepped up
to the plate when I needed a dad in my life. I'll tell you a
little secret.I think he needed me too!

There are other times that we just go riding around and say nothing at all. We turn up the music and listen. We go up and down the street just enjoying our music and each other.
We like a lot of the same songs.

Sometimes Dad and I don't really do anything except talk. I love talking to my dad. He likes to hear what I have to say. I like listening to him too. Some people talk but don't listen. Some people listen but don't talk. We both like to talk and listen so it works out perfect.

Dad and I like to have special time together.
About twice a month or so he takes me
to the movies. That's always a lot of fun.
We pick one out that we both like.
That's really easy to do.
We have a lot in common.
We like many of the same things.

When my mom married my dad,
I was only two years old.
I don't really remember that day.
I've been told all about it though.
My dad read something to me that
said he accepts me and will love me
forever. From then on, I called him "DaDa".

Dad is really super fun to play video games with. We have a blast when we do. Once in a while we go up to Game Stop and buy new games. Then we come home and play them together. That's really fun! And don't think he lets me beat him. If I win it has to be fair and square. That makes me try even harder

My dad is teaching me how to be a man.
Together we do grown up stuff. We
sometimes go to the barber shop. He
gets his hair lined up. I get mine
cut or lined up too. It's nice to
have dad go with me. I'm really proud
of my dad. He works really hard to
provide for me and my mom.

Growing up means doing some things you don't want to do. Dad is helping me learn about that. I had to get glasses and didn't want to wear them. Dad pointed to his own glasses. He told me it's no big deal. Glasses help you to see. Now I actually kind of like wearing them. I really want to be like my dad. I think it's kind of cool that we both wear glasses.

Dad and I go to the store together too.
 I love shopping with my dad. Sometimes
he buys me new sneakers like Jordan's or Nikes.
 Even if he didn't buy me anything,
I would still like shopping with him.
 I just like it when we hang out.

My dad encourages me to follow my dreams. He says I can be anything I want to be. I believe him because he always tells me the truth, no matter what.

The truth of the matter is that
I love doing anything with my dad.
Or, doing nothing at all. I just
love my dad. And…he loves me right back.

I feel really lucky to have my step-dad. Real dads are kind of stuck with the kid they get but step-dads get to choose theirs. I am glad my step-dad chose me and my mom.

Maybe you have a step-dad like I do. Sometimes you may feel sad because he's your step and not your real dad. But step is just a word. If you ask me, step-dads are a step. They step up so they can help us step up and be the best we can be.

Anyone can be a dad. But it takes someone extra special to be a step-dad. Step-dads didn't give us life but they sure make life a whole lot better.

About the Author

Hi! My name is Jarvis. I'm eight years old. I love to do fun things like cook. If you haven't seen my cookbook yet, be sure to check it out. You might wonder what an eight year old boy is doing writing a book. Well, you might say I've got a great imagination. This book is about being an only child. Because I'm an only child in my house, I use my imagination a lot.

Jarvis

CHECK OUT MY OTHER BOOKS

50546039R00015

Made in the USA
Columbia, SC
08 February 2019